We Are All Beautifully Different

We Are All Beautifully Different

An Anti-Bullying Book for Young Children

Written by Jennifer Kempner, MSW

Illustrated by Mish Fornal

Epigraph Publishing Service
Rhinebeck, New York

Book design: Danielle Ferrara

Library of Congress Control Number: 2013955810
ISBN: 978-1-936940-65-3

Epigraph Books
22 East Market Street, Suite 304
Rhinebeck, NY 12572

Printed in the United States of America

This book is dedicated to my daughter Maria
with Love and Gratitude for what she has taught me.

This book is designed to initiate conversations between children
and adults about how it feels for children to be treated
unkindly by other children for whatever the reason. Please use
this book to teach your children how they would feel if they
were in these situations. Ask them the questions and guide
them to a conversation about right and wrong ways to handle
these scenarios.

Thank you for reading this book.
Together we can make a change for our children.

Jennifer Kempner, LCSWR

Foreword

Every child is special. Every child is precious. Every child is unique.

As a physician who has spent his professional career caring for children with cardiac conditions, these descriptions of children have become the essence of my daily life. When my field of medicine - Pediatric Cardiology- started in the 1950's thru the 1960's, many of the surviving infants and children were considered handicapped and "different." As many of my adult patients who grew up in this era have testified, childhood was rough and they were often picked on or ostracized by their childhood peers. Even those adults who were in supervisory positions, such as teachers, coaches and even other doctors, treated them as "not normal." Because some of these people also have other medical conditions or syndromes, this negative interaction with others are often amplified. After all these years, one would assume and hope that this does not occur anymore today. However, the truth is that these misconceptions are still prevalent. As with other forms of bullying, this can be even worse given the technological ability to amplify these misguided behaviors on the Internet.

Over my 15 years of practice, I have come to understand that each child brings special qualities to my life, their family and the community as a whole. Without them, it is we who are "at risk" or handicapped. Without them, it is society which is vulnerable to losing its humanity.

Every day I experience evidence of these truths. However, amongst my experiences, one case stands out. A mother who was followed during pregnancy while she carried a fetus with a complex congenital heart defect known as Hypoplastic Left Heart Syndrome, was advised by doctors, family and friends to abort this fetus since it would not be "normal," require multiple complex heart surgeries and may be intellectually delayed. Despite all this pressure, the mother held to her conviction that this child was special and deserved to have a chance at life. She would do all she could to guarantee this and she did. When her son was about 4 years old, after 3 successful major operations, they were living in a multiple story apartment complex. The child was now quite active and vocal with some physical and mild intellectual delays for which his mother pursued aggressive rehabilitation therapies. One night as they were sleeping, her son awoke her at about 3 am to tell her that he smelt something burning. The mother agreed and became alarmed. She instructed him to knock on the doors of the neighbors on the first floor immediately to notify them, and then to take his younger sister out to the parking lot and wait for her as she called the fire company and notified the other neighbors on the top floors. As all of the residents waited in the parking lot safe and sound, they watched the whole building burn to the ground despite the fire company's best efforts. Everyone survived. None of them ever question whether or not this special child should have been born or not- they know they may not be alive without him.

As I have read this special book written by one of my patients and her mother, I remain honored to have been asked to contribute this small foreword. Maria, like my other patients, has brought a great deal of joy and wonder to my life. In this storybook about our differences and bullying, she and her mother are providing their personal insight and wisdom for countless others. Clearly, their lives together and the message they send, will enrich the readers' lives and stand as a testament to what we all can do when we see the beauty and power in our differences instead of approaching them negatively and destructively. I wish you the reader as much joy in reading this story as I have pride in the young author and her mother for their contribution to our lives.

Eric D. Fethke, MD
Associate Professor of Pediatrics, The Albert Einstein University
Attending Physician, The Children's Hospital at Montefiore
New York

Maria's Story

My 8 year-old daughter, Maria, is my inspiration for writing this book. At the age of 6 months she was diagnosed with a rare genetic disorder called Turner syndrome. According to NORD (National Organization for Rare Disorders)[1] 1 out of 2,000 to 2,500 live female births are diagnosed with Turner syndrome. Turner Syndrome Society of the United States (TSSUS)[2] now estimates the figure to be 1 out of 2,000 live births. Regardless of the numbers, most embryos or fetuses will not survive until birth because they typically abort.

Maria is my miracle child who faces a life-long list of challenges, from medical to social. Like many Turner's kids, Maria loves being social and interacting with others, but she lacks the social skills to do so effectively. She has a difficult time understanding and interpreting facial cues and body language, and she struggles with putting together social dialogue. Unfortunately, it takes a lot of practice to learn the social basics for many Turner's children like Maria.

When Maria was younger she had friends in our neighborhood, but once the other children matured socially, she could not keep up. The children began to ignore her, run away from her and say means things to her. I witnessed many of these incidents but felt powerless to teach the other children about how children can be "different" but still be fun to play with. As Maria got older her self-esteem worsened and she stopped wanting to take the bus to school with the other kids.

I became increasingly depressed as I watched Maria's struggles. I couldn't understand why the other parents in the neighborhood would not intervene and explain to their children that Maria had a disorder and it's ok to play with her. Why didn't the parents ask their children "would you like to be treated that way?" I finally decided something must be done to bring awareness to other parents and shed light on the increasingly present problem of social stigmas and "bullying." My hope is that this book helps Maria and other children in similar situations.

Jennifer Kempner, MSW
Maria's mother

To be clear, not all girls with Turner's have the same social difficulties, as this chromosomal abnormality leads to different issues for each child. For more information on this condition please check out TSSUS.org.

---

[1] www.rarediseases.org

[2] www.turnersyndrome.org

Hi, this is Maria.

Maria's cousins just moved into town and are going to school for the first time today, but things have not been so easy for them. They are feeling different from all the other kids.

1

Hi, this is Cousin Danny.

Today is his first day of school but he cannot fit on the bus.
He feels sad because the other kids are pointing at him and laughing.

Do you think it is nice to point and laugh because Danny can't fit on the bus?

4

Hi, this is Cousin Judy.

She is sitting all by herself on the bus and no one is talking to her.

Do you think it is polite for the other kids on the bus to ignore her?

What could you or your friends do so Judy does not feel so ignored and alone?

EMERGENCY

EXIT

6

Hi, this is Cousin Jack.

He wants to play basketball but he is having a difficult time because he has no hands.

Do you think it is kind for the other kids to make fun of him because he has no hands?

Can you think of any way the team could include Jack in the game?

8

Hi, this is Cousin Alfonzo.

He can't eat some of things that the other kids can eat and he needs to be careful about being near certain foods because he can get sick.

Do you think it is nice to call him weird?

In what way could the kids make it easier for Alfonzo to be a part of the lunch group?

Hi, this is Cousin Jill.

She is too short to reach the book on the shelf in the library. The other kids call her "Shorty" and "Pipsqueak" instead of helping.

Is it okay to call other kids names for being too short or tall?

How could you help Jill do things that are a little hard for her?

Hi, this is Cousin Joey.

He is having trouble sitting still and he can't seem to stop knocking things over or bumping into them. He is making a mess everywhere.

Everyone is getting distracted by him.

Is it possible that it could be hard for Joey to control his movements?

Can you see that Joey is not doing this on purpose?

14

Hi, this is Cousin Betsy.

She is alone at Recess because no one else will play with her. Everyone else is playing tag and hopscotch. No one invites her to join in.

If someone is alone at recess or at a playground, do you think it would be nice to invite them to play?

What could you say to Betsy to help her feel included?

If you were Maria, and you saw your cousins being treated this way,

what would you do?

18

Maybe we could all play together?

19

20

Together We Are All

Beautifully Different!

22

Additional Discussion Questions

1. Has there ever been a time when you felt bullied?
- How did it make you feel?
- How did you handle the situation?
- Did you do or say anything to anyone?

2. Have you ever seen anyone being bullied?
- How did you feel watching it happen?
- Did you say anything to anyone about it?

3. Did you know that when a person is purposely excluded on a regular basis from a group, play activities, or discussion, it can be considered a form of bullying?

4. Did you know that making fun of someone because of his/her skin color, religion, nationality or disability, or anything else that could be perceived as "different," is a form of bullying?

5. Now that you may have a better understanding of what bullying is, have you ever bullied anyone without realizing it?

Social Skills Tips For Parents And Young Children (Ages 5 To 9 Years)

1. **WHAT IS THE DEFINITION OF BULLYING?** Bullying has been defined by the U.S Department of Education as unwanted, aggressive behavior among school-aged children that involves a real or perceived power imbalance. Bullying can be acted out through various methods--verbally, socially and physically.

23

a. **Verbal Bullying** examples include name-calling, teasing, taunting and verbal threats to cause harm.
b. **Social Bullying** examples included ostracizing, repeated exclusion of others on purpose, spreading rumors, telling others not to be friends with someone and embarrassing someone in public.
c. **Physical Bullying** examples include hitting, punching, shoving, pinching, tripping, pushing, taking or breaking someone's things and making mean or rude hand gestures.

These examples are typically repeated and done with bad intent. Note that certain actions are, of course, subject to personal interpretation.

2. **WHAT CAN I DO AS A PARENT IF MY CHILD IS BEING BULLIED IN SCHOOL?** Start by talking with your child to see if anything serious has occurred. Bullying is serious if it has caused any physical or emotional harm that has impacted your child to the point where he/she feels uncomfortable or unsafe. Sometimes events are misinterpreted and no harm was intended, and a child offender simply needs to be reminded of how his/her words or actions can affect others. Ultimately, it is up to the school to determine if an incident constitutes "bullying." If you have any concern that your child is being bullied do not hesitate to contact a teacher, social worker or other official at your child's school as soon as possible.

3. **WHAT CAN I DO IF MY CHILD IS BEING BULLIED IN MY NEIGHBORHOOD?** In the situation where you have not witnessed the "bullying" incident towards your child, it is important to first find out as much information as you can from your child about what has happened. Sometimes more clarification is needed and you may need to speak to the other child or that child's parents (your choice will depend on the age of the other child, how well you know the other child and how well you know the other child's parents). If you witness the "bullying" incident, you should immediately intervene. Possible actions include removing your child from the "bullying" situation and/or modeling proper behavior in front of the "bullying" child. If possible, try to contact the parents of the "bullying" child to discuss the incident; a personal visit or telephone call is best, but an email or letter is also effective. Often parents of a child who bullies other children are not aware of this behavior unless it is brought to their attention. Some parents, however, are not open to hearing negative things about their children, so it is important to be calm and non-accusatory when reaching out to parents of other children in this situation.

---

[3]http://p1232.nysed.gov/dignityact/rgappendixa.html

4. **HOW CAN I TEACH MY CHILD TO DEAL WITH THE EMOTIONS AND FEELINGS ABOUT OTHER KIDS TREATING THEM DIFFERENTLY?** As soon as your child is old enough to understand that he/she is being treated differently it is important to instill in your child that he/she is just as important and wonderful as any other child. If bullying leads to your child becoming withdrawn or having behavioral problems talk to your pediatrician or see a trained child therapist.

5. **HOW CAN I HELP MY CHILD IMPROVE HIS/HER SOCIAL SKILLS?** Most importantly, have an open dialogue with your child about how things are going at school, and in other situations, and let your child know that he/she can share any issues or difficulties with you. You may be surprised about how a little piece of advice may help your child get along better with his/her peers. Check in with your child's school to see if it has any social skills groups that your child can join. Also consider enrolling your child into after-school activities that promote social interaction.

   If your child is having a repeated problem with other children at school, request that a teacher or aide observe your child's interactions with others to document the problems and see if the situation can be improved.

   For parents with children that have Autism or Asperger syndrome, there are trained behavior therapists that can help teach a child on how to appropriately interact with other children in various social situations.

6. **HOW CAN I EXPLAIN TO MY YOUNG CHILD ABOUT OTHER CHILDREN'S DIFFERENCES?** If your child shows interest or concern about why another child is "acting funny" or "looks different," remind your child that everyone is different and if a child looks or acts different it doesn't mean that the child is a bad person, is not nice or is not worthy of being a friend.

7. **HOW MUCH INFORMATION SHOULD I TELL MY CHILD ABOUT "BULLYING" WITHOUT MAKING HIM/HER FEEL SCARED?** Start by explaining to your child that no one has the right to make your child feel bad about himself or herself and let your child know that you are happy and willing to talk to your child at any time about any physically or emotionally uncomfortable situations.

About the Author

Jennifer Kempner, LCSWR

Jennifer Kempner is a mother of three children and a New York State licensed clinical therapist. She received her Master's Degree in Clinical Social Work, specializing in Child and Family Counseling, from Fordham University in New York. She has been working with children, adolescents and adults in various settings since 1999. She currently practices in Dutchess County, New York.

Her personal and professional experiences have led her to write on various topics where the goal is to educate the young, old and in-between, on the different social problems and challenges that many of our children are facing today.

We need to come together as parents, professionals and educators to increase the awareness of the "differences" in many of our children today. We need to teach our children tolerance and acceptance of their peers who are so-called "different." As diagnoses of Autism, ADHD and other syndromes and issues are on the rise, we have no choice but to use awareness and understanding to reinforce empathy in our children. Children that are "different" should not be made to feel like outcasts; they need to be understood, not shunned or ignored.

I would like to give a special "Thank You" to the staff at my daughter's school, Beekman Elementary, which is part of the Arlington Central School District in Dutchess County, New York, for their exceptional efforts in helping my daughter feel more socially supported and emotionally safe while attending school.

Sincerely,
Jennifer Kempner, LCSWR
HealingatHeart.com

---

[4]http://health.usnews.com/health-news/family-health/brain-and-behavior/articles/2011/05/23/us-rates-of-autism-adhd-continue-to-rise-report

About the Illustrator

Mish Fornal

Mish studied at the Art Institute of Fort Lauderdale Florida and at the School of Visual Arts of NYC. Her illustrations represent the love she experienced in her childhood. Mish now lives in Marlboro, New York with her partner, Dale, and children Pheebee and Cooper. Mish can be found on Facebook under Mish Fornal and Sweet Sketches. She dedicates the pictures from this book to her mom and dad who have given infinite support in every aspect of her life.

References

1. *www.rarediseases.org*
2. *www.turnersyndrome.org*
3. *http://p1232.nysed.gov/dignityact/rgappendixa.html*
4. *http://health.usnews.com/health-news/family-health/brain-and-behavior/articles/2011/05/23/us-rates-of-autism-adhd-continue-to-rise-report*

Resources

www.STOPBULLYING.GOV
www.ANTIBULLYING.NET
www.BULLYFREE.COM
www.BULLYINGSTATISTICS.ORG
www.DOSOMETHING.ORG